A B C D E
F G H I
J K L M N
O P Q R S
T U V W
X Y Z

Say Cheese!
A to Z

By Karen Richards Toothaker

Illustrations by Michele Katz

IN YOUR HEART
BOOKS

I, Annabella Tessa Regina, have my very own camera. I take pictures of what I like best from A to Z!

I say, "Say Cheese!" every time

and when I push the button my camera goes, CLICK!

I made my very own book with my very own A to Z pictures – it is the very best picture book ever! Want to see?

ABCs
By
Annabella Tessa Regina

A - my Animals

Say Cheese!

CLICK!

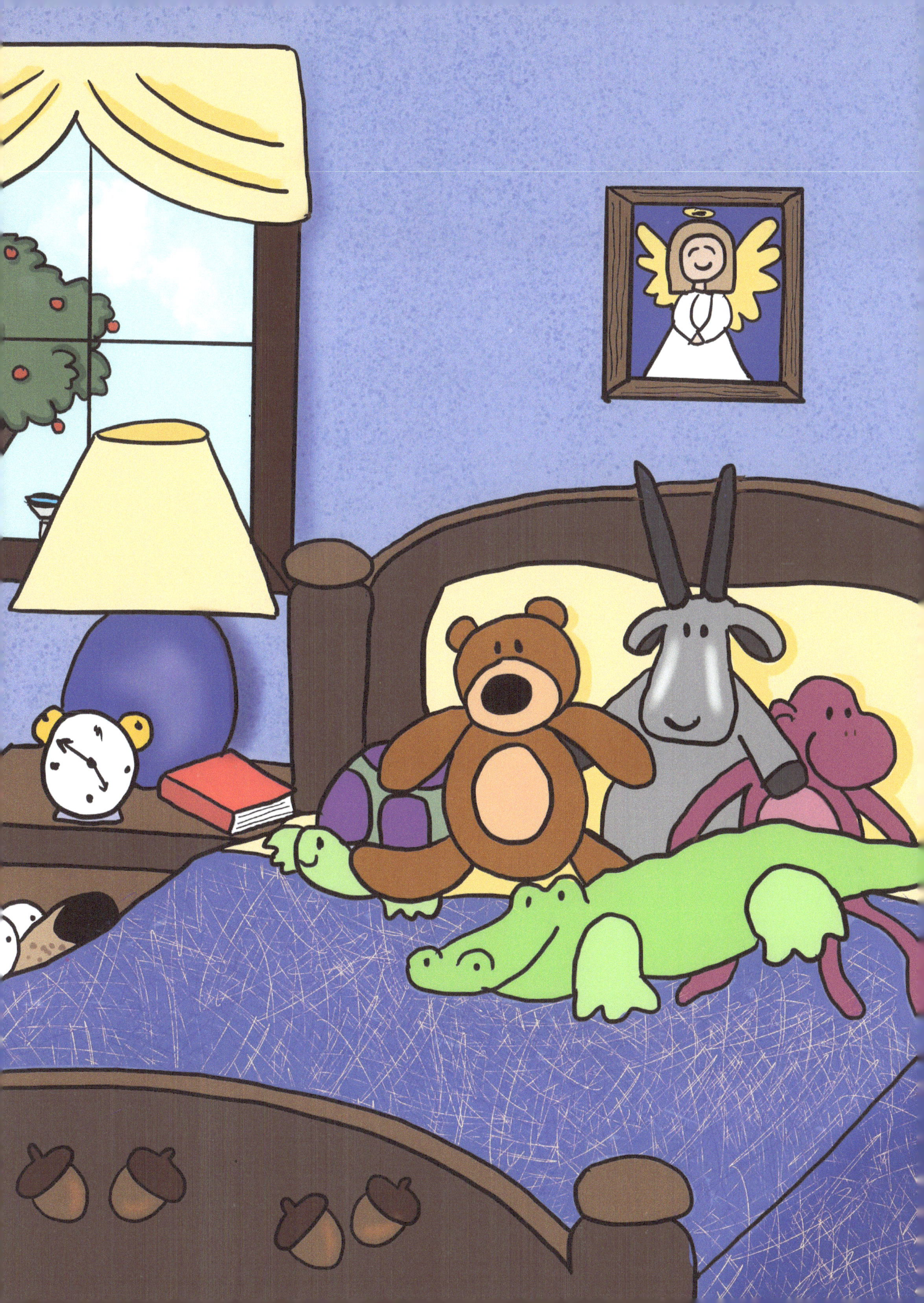

B - Bubbles

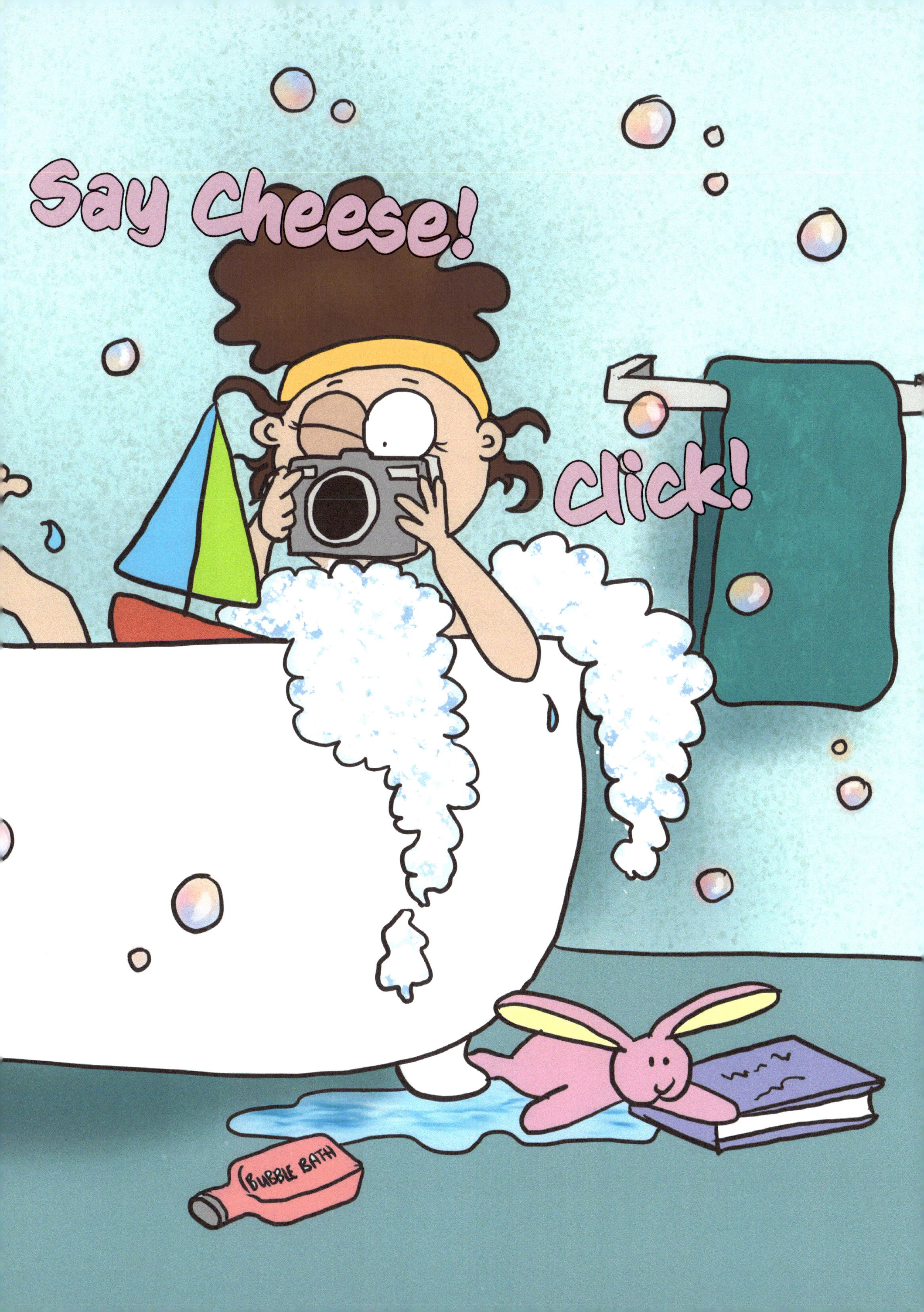
Say Cheese!
Click!
BUBBLE BATH

C Cheese

D my Door

E

Envelopes

F

my Fingers

Say Cheese! Click!

G - Gingerbread

Say Cheese!

cookies

Click!

H
my Hideout

I
Ice cream

J

Jelly beans

K

My Kitchen

Say Cheese! Click!

L - Library

Say Cheese!

Click!

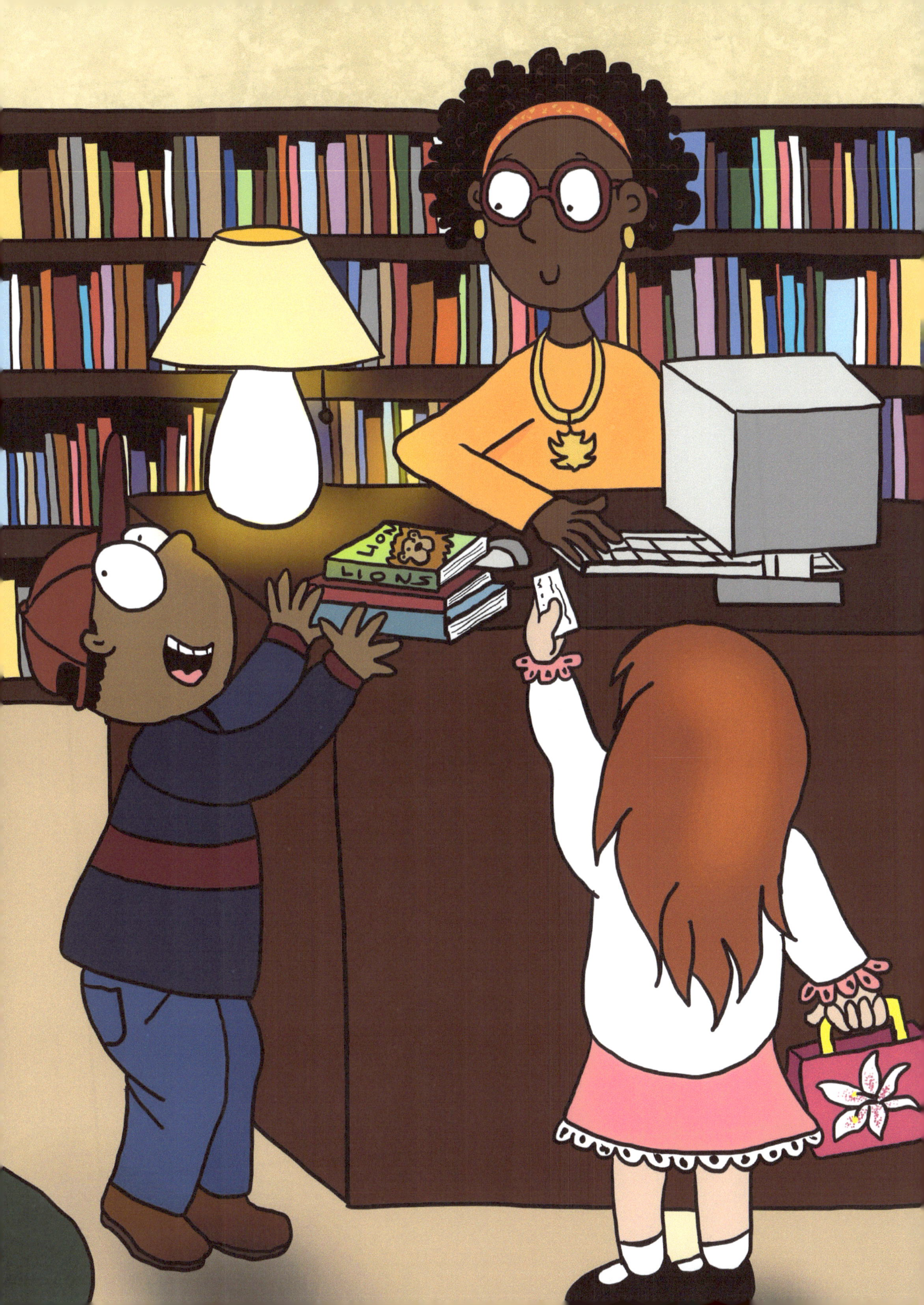
LIONS

M

My Mom's Makeup

N

Numbers

O

my Oatmeal

Say Cheese! Click!

P - Puddles

Say Cheese!

Click!

all my Quarters

R

Roller coaster

Say Cheese!
Click!

S Snow

T Teeth

U underwear

V Valentines

Say Cheese! Click!

W - my Window

Say Cheese! Click!

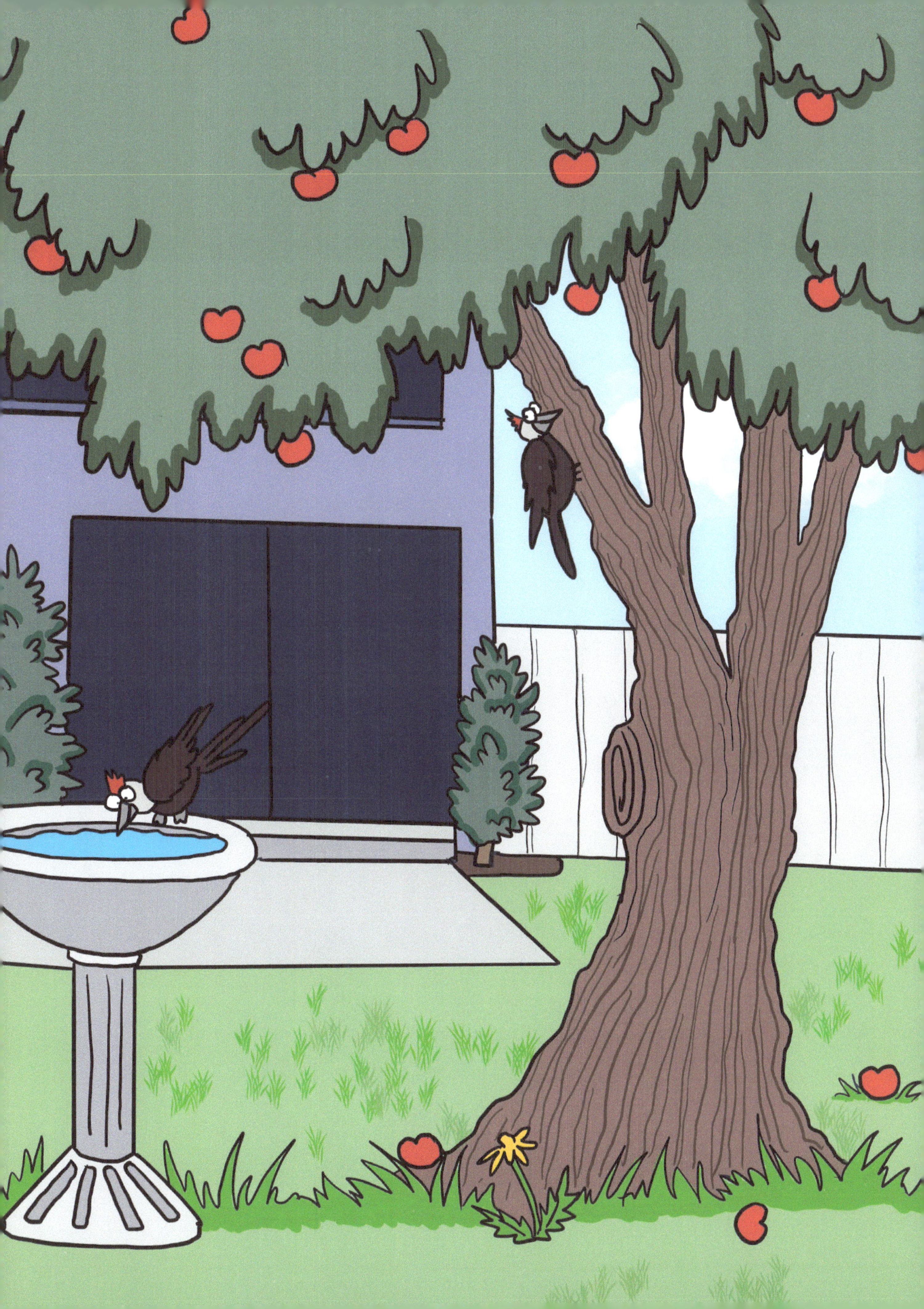

X

my puppy, Xavier

Y

Yams

Z

ZOO

ZEBRA DIET
- GRASS
- HAY
- ALFALFA
- WATER

SPECIAL TREAT - ZUCCHINI

Mom's Zig-Zag shirt

Say Cheese! Click!

See? Don't you agree?
It is the very best picture book ever!
A to Z by me,
Annabella Tessa Regina!

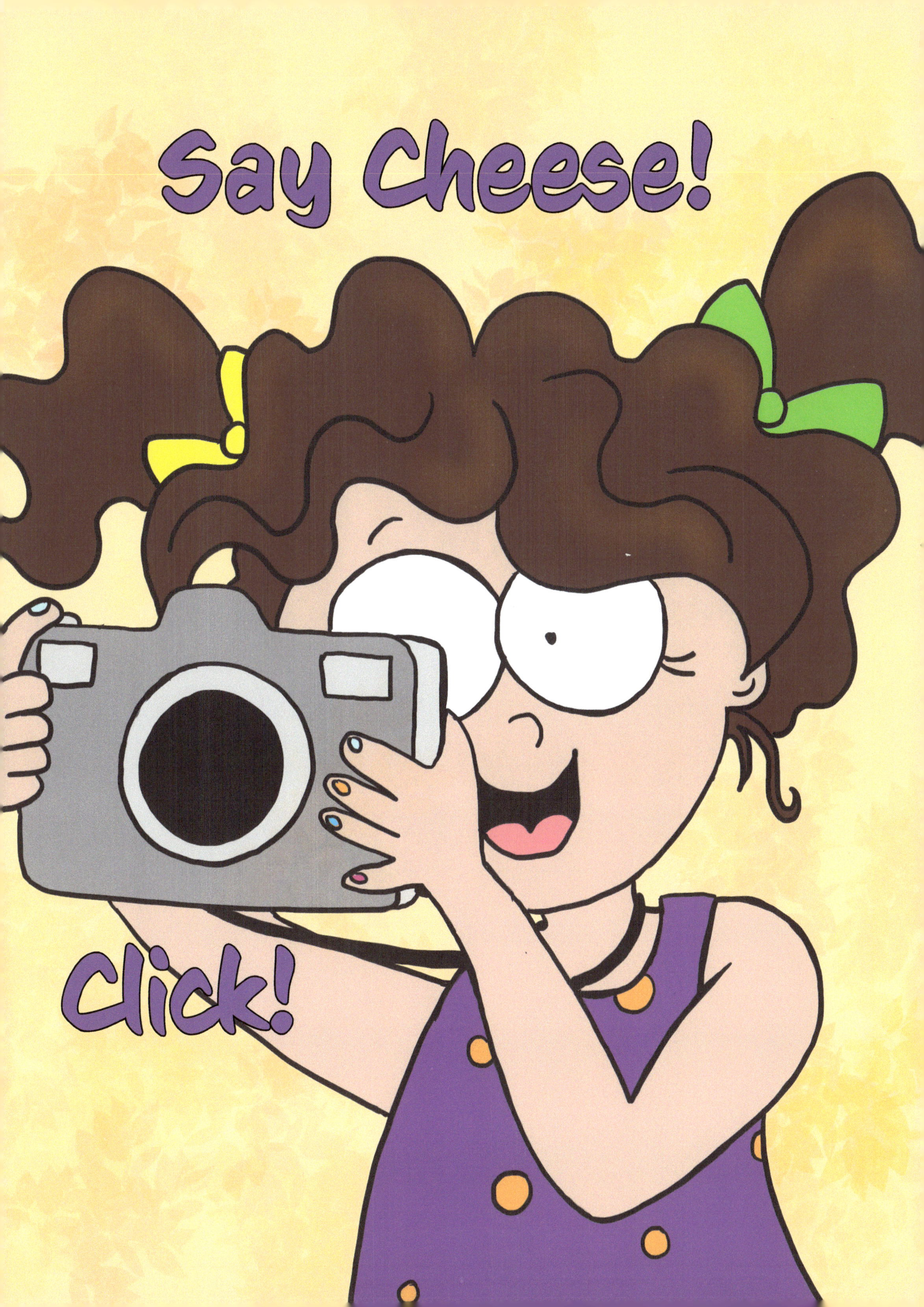
Say Cheese!
Click!

Play A to Z Hide & Seek!
Take another look at each letter A to Z, see if you can find:

A - Annabella, Alligator, Antelope, Apple Tree, Acorns, Alarm Clock, Angel

B - Balloon, Ball, Boat, Bear, Bunny, Book, Bubble Bath, Bath Tub

C - Candles, Cupcakes, Coffee Pot, Cups, Cake, Crackers, Cookies

D - Door, Daisy, Dinosaur, Dolphin, Drawings, Daffodil, Dog, Doll

E - Eagle, Easter Egg, Elephant, Elizabeth, Earth

F - Flowers, Fish, Fern, Frog , the color Fuchsia

G - Grandparents, Glasses, the color Green, Gifts, Garland, Guitar, Gray Hair, Grapes, Giraffe

H - Hockey stick, Hairbrush, Highchair, Helicopter, Hula Hoop, Hat, Hobby Horse, Home

I - Instruments, the color Indigo

J - Jam, Jump rope, Juggling set, Jet

K - Kettle, Kite, Kitten, Keys, Ketchup

L - Laughing, Librarian, Lamp, Lemons, Lunchbox, Lily, Ladder, Leaf, Lion, Lettuce, Lace

M - Mirror, Mom, Mouth, Me, Mad

N - Neighborhood, Newspapers, Nest, Nut, Nose

O - Orange juice, Oval, Octopus, Owls

P - Polka Dots, Puppy, Patch, Pigeon, Pail, Pig, Poncho, the color purple

Q - Quartz, Question mark, Quin

R - Rollercoaster, Rhinoceros, Rabbit, Raccoon, Rocket, the color Red

S - Snowman, Swing, Slide, Shovel, Scarf, Sun, Sticks, Stars

T - Taco, Tie, Toes, Tea, Tray, Table

U - Underwear, Umbrellas, Unicorn

V - Violin, Violets, Vincent

W - Woodpecker, Weeds, Wheel, Wheelbarrow, Water, Watering can

X - Xylophone

Y - Yellow, Yum

Z - Zoo, Zipper, Zebra, Zucchini

Go to www.inyourheartbooks.com
for more Hide & Seek fun and a free printable curriculum guide

Published by In Your Heart Books

Copyright©2022 by Karen Richards Toothaker All rights reserved.

Hard Cover ISBN: 979-8-9862841-1-8

Library of Congress Control Number: 2022914855

No part of this publication may be reproduced, distributed, or transmitted in any form or by any means, including photocopying, recording, or other electronic or mechanical methods, without the prior written permission of the publisher, except in the case of brief quotations embodied in critical reviews and certain other noncommercial uses permitted by copyright law.

This is a work of fiction. Names, characters, businesses, places, events, and incidents are either the products of the author's imagination or used in a fictitious manner. Any resemblance to actual persons, living or dead, or actual events is purely coincidental.

Illustrations by Michele Katz

Book design by Clif Graves of Hinterlandspress.com

Karen Richards Toothaker

As a veteran early childhood educator, author Karen Richards Toothaker experienced first hand the interest and humor of young children. Say Cheese! A to Z is inspired by the children she worked with and by the photos her three very own children took with their very own cameras.

Back in the days when cameras used rolls of film, Karen had her very own Pentax K1000. She no longer uses that camera but still enjoys taking pictures of what she likes best. She has always wondered why we say "Say Cheese!" every time we take a picture. How did it all start?

Visit her at www.inyourheartbooks.com

Dedication:
To my grandchildren, Otis, Natalie, Nolan, Alice, Wesley, Anders, Margaret, and Elizabeth.

You are the very best ever!

Michele Katz (Grieder)

Illustrator, Michele Katz (Grieder) knew she wanted a career creating images for picture books when she was just 7 years old. She earned a Bachelor of Fine Arts degree in illustration from Syracuse University and is a longtime member of SCBWI. She loves to create whimsical, expressive characters and art that makes people smile. Originally from Massachusetts, Michele now lives in Connecticut with her husband and pet turtle and hamster.

Follow her on Instagram @creationsbymit

Dedication:
"To C: My number one fan and favorite letter of the alphabet."